MOMENTS

MOMENTS

COLLATED VERSE

Keith and Elizabeth Stanley-Mallett

ARTHUR H. STOCKWELL LTD
Torrs Park, Ilfracombe, Devon, EX34 8BA
Established 1898
www.ahstockwell.co.uk

© Keith & Elizabeth Stanley-Mallett, 2015
First published in Great Britain, 2015
All rights reserved.
*No part of this publication may be reproduced
or transmitted in any form or by any means,
electronic or mechanical, including photocopy,
recording, or any information storage and
retrieval system, without permission
in writing from the copyright holder.*

*British Library Cataloguing-in-Publication Data.
A catalogue record for this book is available
from the British Library.*

ISBN 978-0-7223-4600-6 Cloth-bound edition.
ISBN 978-0-7223-4601-3 Paperback edition.
*Printed in Great Britain by
Arthur H. Stockwell Ltd
Torrs Park   Ilfracombe
Devon   EX34 8BA*

Previously published poems by the same author:
Little Traveller – Pumpkin Publications
Conspiracy of Faculties – Poetry Now, Forward Press, 1994
Yielding Forms – Poetry Now, 1994
One, That are We – Poetry Now, 1994
Two Minutes of Silence – Anchor Books, 1994
A Norfolk Winter Sunset – Poets England Series, Brentham Press, 1994
Come Silently to Me – Poetry Now, 1995
To the Eye – Poetry Now, 1995
World Wide Conceded Nationally – Poetry Now, 1996
Three Times Twenty – Poetry Now, 1996
I Believe in Betjeman – Poetry Now, 1996
Emotive Machine – Poetry Now, 1996
Essence of Time – Poetry Now, 1996
Poetic Visions – Poetry Now, 1996
Once Upon a Time – Poetry Now, 1996
The Red Fox – Anchor Books, 1997
Soul Winds – Poetry Now, 1997
Across a Timeless Threshold – Anchor Books, 1999
Mrs Batholomew's Door – Anchor Books, 1999
Electronic Life – United Press, 1999
Under An Indigo Moon – Arthur H. Stockwell Ltd, 2009
Beneath Rose-Lemon Skies – Arthur H. Stockwell Ltd, 2009
Before the Rainbow Fades – Arthur H. Stockwell Ltd, 2010
Between Night and Dancing Light – Arthur H. Stockwell Ltd, 2010
Beyond the Last Horizon – Arthur H. Stockwell Ltd, 2010
Upon a Past and Future Path – Arthur H. Stockwell Ltd, 2011
Odd Wit and Other Bits – Arthur H. Stockwell Ltd, 2011
Gilded Images – Arthur H. Stockwell Ltd, 2012
Flies Now The Spirit – Arthur H. Stockwell Ltd, 2013

FOREWORD

BOOK X

To all who read this book of verse we sincerely hope you will enjoy it.

As stated earlier, we did not intend writing a further book but the idea grew stronger in our minds. Thus, here we present *Moments*.

Keith Stanley-Mallett

Here we have put together another volume of verse. We have again cooperated bringing our individual yet complimentary views to bear on our work. So, along with my husband I would like to present this book of poetry entitled *Moments*.

Elizabeth Stanley-Mallett

INTRODUCTION

In our last book, *Flies Now The Spirit*, in the introduction it stated that this title would be our last and final work.

Well, we were wrong, we still had ideas for poetic work and so should have waited. Also, we would like to express our thanks to the production team for publishing this last work in the manner and expertise carried out with our former work.

Keith Stanley-Mallett

It is said it is a woman's privilege to change her mind, well I have certainly changed mine.

With old age comes the urge to do something, so I began writing again. Writing and creating poetry ideally fills that gap. A very pleasurable task indeed, to be able to write *Moments*.

Our latest book is a little different from previous works.

Elizabeth Stanley-Mallett

Part I

Collated Verse

By

Keith Stanley-Mallett

CONTENTS

All That	13
Wisdom	14
Deception	15
One Day	16
'Twixt Heaven and Earth	17
Both Earth and Sky	18
The Probes	19
Love's Imperfections	20
To Live Again	21
Inconsistency	22
Fresh In Bloom	23
Yes	24
Perfection	25
Spring	26
Idiosyncratic Being	27
One Moment	28
Nature's Time	29
Of Spark and Flame	30
Until	31
Diversity	32
Unremitting	33
Fame or Gold	34
Incidentals	35
Sky Scapes	36
Opposites	37
Upon the Cusp	38
Sunday Morning	39
Eternal Light	40
Diverse Reality	41
Youthful Days	42
'Til The Morn	43
Moments	44
As Summer's Land Unfolds	45
Many Things	46
The Timeless Ones	47
The Question	48
Called Again	49

Ghosts	50
Time To Stop	51
Spiritual Worth	52
Forceful Winds	53
Power	54
Reality	55
In Harmony	56
How or When	57
Starlight	58
The Mask of Ignorance	59
Twilight Time	60
Times	61
Living Essence	62
A Fall of Springtime Rain	63
Final Forms	64
A Visitor	65
Rain	66
Fifty-Five Degrees	67
In Concord?	68
A Short Essay – Time is But a Moment	69

All That

All, that once I saw and knew
    Has gone into that long night,
Or held a spirit, pale seen
    A floating orb of light.

Thus it is with everyone
    No matter history's date,
Good, bad, clever or simple
    We all meet the same fate.

Wisdom

Now a senior citizen
    Eighty years of age,
Looking upon the world's
    Great historic stage.

I see the spirit thus burn bright
    Bringing forth the truth,
Yet with darkness, the shadows
    Fill the mind anew.

For I have seen the history
    Of this island's past,
Lived throughout the warring times
    'Til the present cast.

So now I know humanity
    In its many forms,
And I fear, we have far to go
    'Ere, wisdom is born.

Deception

I look upon the present
    From an age now past,
And now discern the problems
    Such mentality holds fast.

Within a reaching structure
    A political web,
That caught both body and mind
    In all that they did and said.

Yet still they serve up the hash
    In belief the public is blind,
Hiding behind crafted words
    Deceiving the common mind.

How long will it take for truth
    To be spoken by all,
Regardless of hierarchy
    Honesty stands strong and tall.

One Day

Elegance and sincerity
    Once so prominent and smart,
Now belongs to history
    As all that soon departs.

Of gentlemen and ladies
    And highs and lows of elegance,
The smart and the not so smart
    Both a mix of intelligence.

Yet the peoples of England
    Were England's true self,
For without her people
    The country would not do well.

We may have lost elegance
    And positions in the world,
But one day she'll recover
    With her proven right unfurled.

'Twixt Heaven and Earth

Here I stand in sunset's glow
    Under a sky of liquid fire
Such a colourful evening
    A palette exotic to admire.

Yet, time again erases all
    Under a shadowed blanket,
As darkened clouds drift to cover
    The last golden rays of sunset.

Fast the brooding elements
    Gather like witches' black shrouds,
Hiding the face of the moon
    As the wind begins to howl.

Ever darkening, the sky becomes
    Like a devil's cloak thrown wide,
From which ensues the lightning
    To flash so bright and wild.

Thunderous becomes the noise
    Yet not a sign of rain,
So play, the elementals
    'Twixt heaven and earth again.

Both Earth and Sky

As distant echoes on the wind
    Grow faint in memory.
The human voice in many forms
    Fades in timeless air of history.

For unlike melody and song
    That attracts and soothes the mind,
Humanity's voice is converse
    So can irritate in time.

Unlike that of animals
    Or songbirds up on high,
Whose diverse voice and singing
    Enchants both earth and sky.

To hear the rush and break of waves,
    The running murmur of a stream,
Or whispering breeze upon the trees
    Nature's sounds, supreme.

The Probes

Our probes go out
    For years and years,
Landing on a piece of rock
    To which transmissions steer.

The probes are still
    Quite primitive,
Yet findings they can record
    And thus be informative –

For those who need
    To learn and grow,
Scientific knowledge
    We must all seek to know.

Love's Imperfections

To please or not to please
    Is that the question?
Or to anger instil
    Inviting confession!

If such confession's felt,
    Thus anger shown is right,
Yet, perhaps it's jealously
    That augments the fight.

Little tiffs, arguments,
    Can grow and become
Quite out of proportion,
    So, at a loss it leaves one.

Such silliness exists
    'Twixt male and female,
Although it's part of life,
    Thus, love can sometimes fail.

To Live Again

Spring is here once again
    To wake the lands from rest,
Bringing forth the flowers
    Buds and leaves afresh.

Listen to the diverse birds
    A myriad songs and sounds
Filling the morning air
    As nature's life abounds.

The very air smells now so clean,
    And everywhere looks new
Wild fresh green spreads its growth
    And wild flowers drink of dew.

All that lives upon the land
    Lake, river, field or plain
Awake to spring's gentle warmth
    And seek to live again.

Inconsistency

Nothing is consistent
    In this ever-troubled world,
Especially human beings
    As their lives unfurl.

The government says one thing
    Then changes fast its mind,
Stores put up their prices
    Yet sales go down they find.

There's such inconsistency
    Throughout humanity,
On the one hand this or that
    On the other wait and see.

If only we could come
    Together and agree,
Perhaps in peace, move forward
    In enlightenment agree.

Fresh In Bloom

I listen to the metronomic
    Ticking of the clock on the wall,
As I gaze from my window
    On the scene that befalls –

Bathed as now, in warm-lit sunlight
    Each field and tree, each meadow,
Newly showing off their green
    Bordered by a hedgerow.

Above, the clear blue sky of morning
    Glows as a distant coverlet,
Where soft-white drifting cloud
    Moves lazily to the west.

I see the ponies in the high field
    Grazing upon the lush grown grass,
Newborn plants are fresh in bloom
    For spring is here at last.

Yes

Beyond the moon
    Beyond the air,
Beyond the earth
    Beyond all care.

Out into space
    Out into cold,
Out into dark
    Out to be bold.

Into the void
    Into that place,
Into far realms
    Into God's face.

Yes, we will reach,
    Yes, we will try,
Yes, to new worlds
    Yes, we will fly!

Perfection

To hold the perfect palette
    Of colour and tint to blend,
Perfection of a poem
    In the written word to send –

Such meaning to eye and mind
    To lift both spirit and soul,
For in each painted word
    Lies a spark of the whole.

To weave both colour and script
    Needs an artist's touch to lay,
Bringing such true feeling
    From the work to convey –

Emotion written in verse
    Has such meaningful power,
For its beauty and sound
    Touches the heart's sweet bower.

Spring

The weather is changing
    And warmth is returning,
Winter's retreating
    And spring is full yearning –

To burst into strong life
    Into leaf and to bud,
Thrusting through the cold earth
    And frost-covered mud.

For new life is growing
    It's spreading to cover,
All of the countryside
    And gardens with endeavour.

Springtime in England is
    Nature's time for growth
From a weed to a tree
    Spring nourishes them both.

Idiosyncratic Being

Is the apple of her eye
    Equal to the pear of her ears,
Or the carrot of her nose
    The leek, her mouth compares.

For the eye infers an apple
    Is greater than all other,
Thus becomes an imprint
    In the eye, a wonder.

How many silly sayings
    From years of long ago
Are meant from true feeling?
    Or conjured from need to show –

Affection, in a strange way,
    Odd and comic sayings
Abound in our language,
    Idiosyncratic beings.

One Moment

Old time moves on
    And things pass by,
Although 'tis slow
    It does so fly.

Thus we are caught
    In life's concern,
Not privy to such
    That we could learn.

Just swept by tide
    Each night and day,
To live and work
    Or dream and play.

So we with time
    Move fast along,
One moment here
    Next, we are gone.

Nature's Time

The sun is high
    Both hot and bright,
Midday is near
    And all seems right.

Horse and cattle
    Are in their fields,
Roaming, browsing
    As is their will.

Hedge, shrub and tree
    Are leafing new,
For nature's time
    Of birth runs true.

The day is warm
    And birds in flight,
Do wheel and swoop
    Chatter on high.

All now so calm
    So still and right,
Spring once again
    A splendid sight.

Of Spark and Flame

Life is full of work and drear
    And long the hours to keep,
First to come, each child must learn
    With schooling through each week.

Yet fast to maturity
    We quickly come to grow,
Thinking now we've learned so much
    There's not much left to know.

So the years pass quickly on
    In time we become aware,
Within the mind, spark or flame
    Awaits release to share –

Whatever secrets lie there
    For those of wisdom see
Far beyond normality,
    Acquiring truths to free –

Such knowledge, waiting release
    Only given to few,
Who have the spark or the flame
    To bring forth wisdom true.

Until

The evening sun
    From darkened cloud,
Pours forth its rays
    Through enclosing shroud.

That quickly gathers
    Across the sky,
Thus twilight falls
    The quicker by.

Then light does fade
    The sun dips low,
The horizon dims
    To a faint gold glow.

That too, fades away
    Leaving night to stay,
Thus all is darkness
    Until light of day.

Diversity

Folk are so diverse
    Are so different,
One to another
    Do they complement?

Well, it's strange to say
    Such a motley crowd,
Get along so well
    Whether quiet or loud.

No matter who we are
    Our differences
We live, work and play,
    No inferences –

Should be made or writ,
    For diversity
Of one to another
    Creates conversely –

A stronger joining,
    Of kind and of place,
To forward each mind
    And the human race.

Unremitting

Such mist that hangs
    Sore damp and cold,
Blankets the view
    And does enfold –

With rain that falls
    Constant, dripping,
Soaking the scene
    Unremitting.

Drear is the day
    Dull is the mind,
No blue on high
    Or sunlight find.

So turn away
    Both sight and thought,
For other things
    Are better sought.

Fame or Gold

Wither wilt thou wander?
    Is a saying old,
Yet, still true today
    For fame or for gold.

Some try for greatness
    Others are of sin,
Some, men of science
    And of medicine.

Or be a soldier
    Guarding liberty,
Airman or sailor
    In air or on sea.

Then, there are spacemen
    Men of the future,
Where will they wander
    With ship and computer?

Incidentals

Is it incidental
    To behave badly,
Drink and become drunk
    Then to laugh madly.

Perhaps speak out of turn
    Jump to conclusions,
Start an argument
    Arrange confusion.

All are incidental
    And can sometimes occur,
Reactions to life
    Reaching end of tether.

There is always something
    That annoys or creates
Incidental moments,
    Which we all seem to make.

Sky Scapes

The sky hangs luminous,
    A pale grey mist of air.
Above, beyond and low
    Lying, for all to share.

Sometimes lit bright and blue
    By a gold summer sun,
Inviting all to grow
    To reach, for life as one.

Or overcast with rain
    That falls from heavy cloud,
Nature's fresh offering
    To quench life's thirsty crowd.

Thunderous elements
    Can form within the sky,
Bringing concussive noise
    And bright lightning strikes –

Sky scapes dark and light.

Opposites

Black and white or colour
    How should a picture be?
For one is colourful
    The other, sombre see.

Colour gives to the eye
    Nature's own bright array,
Yet, black and white has strength
    Which to the mind conveys.

Diverse in light and shade
    Each is to the other,
Positive, negative
    Thus, opposites of colour.

Each has its rightful place
    Amongst the many arts,
For both portray the truth
    And touch the mind and heart.

Upon the Cusp

Within the early hours
    Betwixt the night and day,
Lies life upon the cusp
    Neither earthly or fa'e.

For 'tis the hour of dreams
    What is, yet, what may be?
Within such drifting thoughts
    Lies the essence perceived.

Therefore, within degrees
    It touches all of life,
Both the high and the low
    Each mind, will seek the why?

Thus, so the night will fade
    As light creeps new at dawn,
Reality steps forth
    As day once more is born.

Sunday Morning

I have awoken to
    A March Sunday morning,
Sunshine bright and windless
    A beautiful day's dawning.

White puffs of cloud ride high
    Within a light blue sky,
Above a green landscape
    From which new leaves imply –

Spring is thus upon us,
    Life thrusts its buds anew,
Reaching, seeking for growth
    With vigour strong and true.

Sunshine glows, lights the land
    And birdsong fills the air,
For spring is upon us
    A time for all to share.

Eternal Light

Shines a diamond star
    Above a crescent moon,
Bright set in the heavens
    As a symbol to view –

Against the black velvet
    Like jewels to admire,
So distant, yet so close
    Gleams this heavenly fire.

Many ages have passed
    For this moon and this star,
Although there are others
    They are brighter by far.

For these shining bodies
    All aglow in the night,
Give beauty upon high
    With their eternal light.

Diverse Reality

Why is it humanity
    Is so strangely diverse?
Not so much by colour
    Or even race inferred.

It is by religion
    Such diversity shared,
Many are the beliefs
    Many beliefs impaired.

There are so many gods
    And goddesses also,
With many an adept
    Whose teachings they follow.

Therefore, cause and effect
    Comes between all who pray,
For each sect is convinced
    Their preaching is the way.

So the conflict unfolds
    Betraying humanity,
Because of religions'
    Diverse reality.

Youthful Days

So many thoughts and memories
    Occur within the seeking mind,
Remembering youthful days
    Of the adventurous kind.

Then, but a short while later
    Find interest in boys or girls,
For it is as ever was
    Childhood fades and youth unfurls.

So to adulthood you come
    Still young of mind but stronger,
'Tis then, time passes faster
    So wish the days were longer.

One thing more I wish to say
    That can be counted upon,
To have such thoughts and memories
    You lived life full and long.

'Til The Morn

For the coming of summer
    Fresh spring prepares the way,
Intermittent warmth and cold
    Defines each dawning day.

'Til the morn the sun does rise
    More bright and more intense,
Heralding summer's return,
    Such times happily spent.

Thus the summer approaches
    And all begin to grow,
Creating nature's beauty
    As we in life do know.

So comes the season, once more
    Sun-bright, hot and lazy,
Across the fields and meadows
    Grey spires, distant, hazy.

Moments

There comes throughout our lives
    Rare and mystic moments,
When we feel, hear or see
    A fleeting change of sense.

Perhaps meandering
    Within a shady wood,
There comes this sense of fa'e
    Strange, then 'tis gone for good.

Or strolling in moonlight
    Beneath a harvest moon,
Suggests an old ash tree
    Will understand your mood.

There are many levels
    Of energies unbound,
That sometimes briefly touch,
    Which to us, is profound.

As Summer's Land Unfolds

April, a time of dampness
    One month ahead of May,
Thus all should welcome April
    And the rain she conveys.

Yet March sees the first to bloom
    So early in the year,
'Tis sun-bright yellow and blue
    With early birdsong, clear.

Then comes the May-time beauty
    With its wild wayside blooms,
Nurtured by sun and rain
    She takes us into June.

A month that is hot and bright
    Turning corn into gold,
Helping all in earth to grow
    As summer's land unfolds.

Many Things

In my study are remnants,
    Objects of days long gone,
Old books, ornaments and clocks
    An oil lamp that once shone.

Bric-a-brac and object d'art
    Pictures, a Guy Fawkes' mask,
And upon my desk there stands
    A large ornate hourglass.

There are thus, so many things
    That nudge the mind to write,
Of both the past and present
    Helping to see the light.

Some may call it a clutter!
    To an extent, that's true,
Yet, through these things around me
    I touch both old and new.

The Timeless Ones

The year continues turning
    Our world upon its course,
Yet the world needs not the year
    Just planetary force.

For all things are in balance
    As they circle the sun,
And do not need months or years
    They are the timeless ones.

A family of planets
    With their circling moons,
Called a solar system
    That from our star was hewn.

So then, the years continue
    The earth spins on its way,
Thus we gain a little more
    In learned thought each day.

The Question

From time to time there occurs
    Such moments in your thoughts,
That almost defy reason
    The question, mind has wrought.

Astronomically vast
    The universe is seen,
And growing yet larger still
    As space expands, it seems.

We are so minute, so small,
    Compared with creation,
Uncountable galaxies
    Energies and fusion.

The whys and the wherefores,
    Each question to answer,
So mankind seeks for the truth
    Now, the future and after.

Called Again

One moment unconscious
    Devoid of life and of thought,
Perhaps for untold ages
    Or just a short while, unsought.

Do thus, spirits exist
    Within some darkened realm?
Awaiting call and touch
    To again taste life, full well.

How long between the ages?
    How long 'twixt life do sleep?
To come again a witness
    For endeavour and for deed.

For we are all of spirit
    And a spirit be in name,
So live your life well and long
    Before you're called again.

Ghosts

Wherever ghosts gather
    Across this old land,
Angry, distressed and lost
    'Ere woman or man!

Now estranged from this world
    Caught in a nether void,
Condemned to haunt,
    Spitefully paranoid.

Hidden well within their realm
    They engender such fear,
By their whispers, bangs and touch
    That you may feel or hear.

'Tis best they are left alone
    Especially at night,
Unless you wish to meet
    And give yourself a fright.

Time To Stop

History is supposed
    To tell when things are wrong,
By attitude and action
    Thus we learn from days gone.

Many the false promises
    Many the evil deeds,
Done in the name of Christ
    Yet 'tis fear, that it feeds.

Also with indifference
    Did monarchs, this country rule,
Torture and beheading
    A time unjust and cruel.

What of battles quickly sought
    Upon a minor pretext,
The slaughter of so many
    Bloodily laid to rest.

Have we learnt from history?
    Have we learnt the lessons?
Do we make the same mistakes?
    'Tis time to stop aggression!

Spiritual Worth

Shadows of the night
    A cloak of darkness presides,
Until clouds depart
    Revealing the moon that rides –

High over the land,
    In a softening white glow,
Treating each feature
    As if all fa'e was on show.

For each phase of the moon
    From crescent to full orb,
In romance and mystery
    She is queen of them all.

For such is our moon
    This satellite of earth,
Time has dictated
    Her spiritual worth.

Forceful Winds

There blows such forceful winds,
    The birds do not fly,
Lifting from branch or hedge
    Are blown through the sky.

Quick and dark are the clouds,
    The trees thrash to and fro,
And spiteful rain lashes
    The flowers, bent low.

Power

Governments lack cohesion
    Especially with people,
Whose knowledge of politics
    Is only fair to feeble.

Their power of auditory
    Does not mean understanding,
They are there by party choice
    And not by comprehending.

Having stated the obvious
    There are those who really care,
I do hope these are the ones
    Whose government they share –

But as is commonly known
    Politicians have power,
I suggest they use it well,
    For this country to flower.

Reality

What is reality?
    What is this life we lead?
What if this life was not
    As real as we believe.

It's so hard to define,
    For we are all a part
Of the make up of life,
    Where do we really start?

Are we thus physical
    Or metaphysical,
Are we just images
    Impressed to recall?

Or is there real substance
    To confirm all is real,
Is reality true?
    Or in league to conceal?

In Harmony

Tick tock, tick tock,
    Tickety tockety
Tickety tockety
    Sound the clocks in harmony.

They tick and tock away
    All the hours night and day,
Measuring all the time
    Where sun and moon display.

Like the sun and the moon
    Who keep great cosmic time,
They copy this passing
    Of moonlight and sunshine.

For each does time convey
    Heavenly or earth day,
They measure large and small
    The passing of moments away.

How or When

History continues
    For it runs all through time,
Ages past to the future
    Lived by humankind.

Years may come, years may go
    Continuous, appears
All that are born and die
    Are subject to its fears.

Life is but a moment
    In living history,
We know not how or when
    Our final destiny.

So we live out our days
    Regardless of the time,
Hoping there is an answer
    Equable, sublime.

Starlight

There are within the heavens
    Far and further still,
Where, in this vast space
    Mystery and beauty fill.

Bright suns, blue, white and yellow
    Pierce the dark'n'd void,
Mighty glowing jewels
    Creating life so employed.

For creation and destruction
    Alternately befalls,
All matter existing
    Throughout time's long-lasting halls.

Thus for each age-old sun
    Collapsing in death,
Comes birth of the new
    With such power and zest.

There is in the heavens
    Such wonderful sights,
The greatest of these
    Is perfected, in starlight.

The Mask of Ignorance

Many a long year the earth
    Has slept beneath a mask,
First, by our ignorance,
    Now by deceit is cast.

A mask of ignorance
    Determined by secrecy,
Such interference of truth,
    In a democracy?

To keep from the people
    These most important facts,
That alien craft and beings
    Are on earth and in contact.

Above and below the ground
    And hidden in our seas,
There's also the incidents
    That occur 'twixt them and we –

The natives of this planet,
    Yet, they are more advanced
And have the power to rule!
    Thus, we must wait and enhance –

Our knowledge and our stance.

Twilight Time

The land lays quiet
    In the soft light
Of evening,
    A tranquil sight.

Melodic song of birds
    Drifts in the still air,
Softly sung finality
    For all to hear and share.

Slowly, the golden light
    Of the setting sun,
Dips behind the trees, and
    Twilight lives as day succumbs.

A natural beauty
    Falls over this quiet land,
As darkening shadows
    Reach out, with night's glove'd hand.

Times

The times we all live in
    Are to us normality,
Whatever the year or date
    Or even the century.

For we are the produce
    Of old time and of place,
We cannot alter this fact
    It is the life we face.

Unknown is timelessness
    For we are of one time,
Yet, should we consider
    Being able to define –

Living life in diverse ways,
    In the past or future,
Or on differing worlds
    With their strange wrought culture.

I think we should refrain
    From such deep, far-reaching thoughts,
And thank reality,
    For normality, unsought.

Living Essence

What is this strange power
    This living essence supreme?
That is the spark of life
    In all that lives and breathes.

Wherein its purest form
    Does this essence reside,
All, or just part of mankind,
    Those who care, does it abide?

For in this earth's great crowd
    There is both good and evil,
Thus the spirit has flown
    From those who torture and kill.

Yet this spiritual essence
    In many forms, does show,
It lies within the human soul
    With all who care, their spirit grows.

A Fall of Springtime Rain

Puddles left in the night
    From a fall of springtime rain,
Shimmer and catch the light
    As morning touches the lane.

Each hedgerow, tree and shrub
    Have drunk their refreshing fill,
As have the plants in tubs
    In valley and upon hill.

Soon the days will lengthen
    For all, quick to take their fill,
And the sun will strengthen
    In valley and upon hill.

Puddles form in the night
    Gathered from fresh springtime rain,
Shimmering in sunlight
    As shadows leave the lane.

Final Forms

Indefinable passing
    Of existence for all,
Unaccountable fauna
    And diverse flora, fall –

From nature's guiding hand
    Over long millennia
Of earth-wrought living cells,
    And life-forming endeavour.

So onwards through vast ages
    Creation and extinction,
Seeking the final forms
    For earth-bound life's completion.

Through all this mighty sequence
    Are we finally at an end,
Or, is this living process
    Continuing, faults to mend?

A Visitor

We have a wild visitor
    Who arrives without a sound,
A beautiful vixen
    A little after sundown.

Quickly crossing the lawn
    To where we leave some food,
She nervously looks around
    Full knowing she intrudes –

Then rapidly downs her meal
    And takes the biscuits left,
Trotting back across the lawn
    Perhaps to her den to rest.

I hope to see her often
    For I know she has few friends,
A fox can be delightful
    As all should comprehend.

Rain

I can't see out the window
    No, I can't see any more,
The rain just falls in torrents
    And continues just to pour.
Then daylight slowly dims
    To a miserable sight,
Becoming so depressing
    It feels almost like night.
So what is there to do?
    Light the lamp and read a book?
Or be just like the weather
    Miserable and forsook!

Fifty-Five Degrees

Fifty-five degrees
    Reads the thermometer,
It's getting warmer
    As we leave cold winter.

There's still a while yet
    To go, before it's warm,
To see a sky of blue
    Where soft white clouds do form –

Floating high on winds
    That gently touch and flow,
And all on land is green
    As nature's life does grow.

So, here I now wait
    In fifty-five degrees,
Waiting for warm days
    And summer's balm to please.

In Concord?

Singularly attractive
    As monumentally ugly,
The totality of
    This entire humanity –

Never ceases to surprise,
    With never a single thought
Of using intelligence,
    The human race is fraught –

With rival intentions
    Of one versus another,
Diverse nations thus repeat
    Setting man against brother.

'Tis long since, time they learnt,
    To act as one in concord,
Stop the silly bickering
    And reap the great reward.

A Short Essay

Time is But a Moment

It took but a moment, so says the scientific world, to create the universe, in so doing, began a time of never-ending moments.

Each moment of creation strung like beads on a string, almost never ending until that moment of time when the universe finally destructs. So not only ending all matter but also time.

Just like everything else in the universe, time travels in evolving circles or orbits. Just as planets die and become fragmented and suns collapse or explode, both in fullness of time merge their fragmented parts and gases etc., to become again that from which they came.

Thus, why should not time, slowly rotating, itself becoming fragmentary in force, with less effective movement of time. So as total reality in all forms subsides and dissipates only to strengthen again as it completes the circle or orbit of space-time awareness and dimensional flexibility. Therefore, creating once again moments of time, for time is everything. Time is movement ie moments.

Part II

Collated Verse

By

Elizabeth Stanley-Mallett

Previously published poems by the same author:
  Guiding Star – Forward Press, 2009
  Winter Sun – Forward Press, 2009
  Beneath Rose-Lemon Skies – Arthur H. Stockwell Ltd, 2009
  A Narrow By-Way – Anchor Books, 2010
  Valentine – Forward Press, 2010
  June Roses – Forward Press, 2010
  Little Green Men – Forward Press, 2010
  Before the Rainbow Fades Part II – Arthur H. Stockwell Ltd, 2010
  Between Night and Dancing Light Part II – Arthur H. Stockwell Ltd, 2010
  Valentine 2010 – Forward Poetry, 2011
  Three to a Seat – Forward Poetry, 2011
  Learners All – Forward Poetry, 2011
  The Door – Arthur H. Stockwell Ltd, 2011

CONTENTS

If Only	77
Always Tomorrow	78
Remembered Evenings	79
Fidget Fingers	80
Companionship	81
Junk Mail	82
Love Songs	83
The Comfort of a Cat	84
Once in a Time	85
Reading and Romance	86
Greetings Cards	87
One a Day	88
The Sty	89
The Tomboy	90
In Time	91
Just Music?	92
Lucky Numbers	93
Sorcery	94
The Drifter	95
The Harvest Field	96
Regrets	97
Redemption	98
Ancestors	99
Dimensions	100
Dead or Alive	101
Earthbound	102
Lady Fox	103
Dew Under the Sun	104
A Parcel	105
Remnants	106
Summer Snow	107
Lollipop Lady	108
Eyes	109
Moon Watch	110
Pipes and Drums	111
Newspapers	112
The Bridge	113

Sunblock	114
Stepping Stones	115
The Thatcher	116
The Milestone	117
Lord of the Manor	118
Diverse Arts	119
Used Cars Salesman	120
The Wheelwright	121
The Old Carpenter	122
The Old Shopkeeper	123
The Village Ironmonger	124
Agricultural Merchants	125
The Chemist	126
Internet Banking	127

If Only

I wish I could adapt my mind
    To once again write in rhyme,
It used to be so easy
    Now I struggle all the time.

My brain still functions well
    Memory as sharp as ever,
What is wrong I ask myself
    Am I now, not clever?

This could be possible
    For I'm no Einstein,
Relax, let the mind work
    Then, all could be just fine.

Wishing to tell the truth
    I marvel at the divine,
I simply cannot comprehend
    A universe sublime.

Always Tomorrow

Why is it always tomorrow
    Why can't it be right now,
I am tired of all the waiting
    I'll find a method somehow.

To bring about quicker routes
    To bring my plans to fruition,
Some matters are so urgent
    They override conditions.

When a child needs a surgeon
    And blood is in short supply,
A donor from the people
    May death's demand deny.

A blazing building roars away
    And cannot wait for rain,
The fireman must NOW attach
    Their hoses to the rising main.

Remembered Evenings

Each evening the air would throb
    Caused by the bombers' noise,
Off in squadrons to Germany
    Our brave RAF boys.

Come the dawn the next day
    They limped back in ones,
Many on fire, bits falling off
    But they had dropped their bombs.

On towns and military targets
    In Germany's heartland,
Halting the mighty war machine
    Of the Führer's evil band.

So they landed back at Little Staughton
    The airfield close to my abode,
Well-earned rest then taking off again
    Skimming the chapel with a full bomb load.

The airfield was busy throughout the war
    When peace came it was stripped quite bare,
Planes flown out and the drome
    Just left to the ghosts lingering there.

Fidget Fingers

I thought I had finished writing
    Now I'm not sure,
My fingers itch to press the keys
    To churn out more and more.

Why can't I keep them still
    Why not let them rest?
For years they've swiftly moved
    Tapping out my best.

I cannot give up writing
    I need to use my brain,
Must not go rusty
    Oil the wheels, create again.

I am pleased with my efforts
    I really enjoy the work,
It is nice to finally realise
    I am not just a berk.

Companionship

Without any siblings to grow with
    I was an only child,
Parents steeped in religion
    I grew a little wild.

There was a baby before me
    But she failed to survive,
Harelip and cleft palette
    Made sure she shortly died.

Romping in the fields when I could
    Without the company of others,
I joined the animals in play
    But had no sister or brother.

Truly on my own, and sad
    I longed for human friends,
My comrades all around me
    Were loads of ducks and hens.

When I found myself a job
    I was no longer isolated,
I loved the intimacy of work and
    Friendships were created.

Junk Mail

It rattles through the letterbox
    Unwanted heaps of trash,
Why do they keep sending
    Marketing ploys so brash?

Just mail-order catalogues
    Depicting the same junk mail,
I surf the Internet to buy
    So their leaflets must fail.

I quickly throw them away
    Stuffed into the bin,
A nuisance piling up
    I feel I cannot win.

To write letters of complaint
    To each individual firm,
The cost of postage alone
    Would take more than I earn.

I like to receive a parcel
    And I read most of the letters,
Though the rest drive me doolally
    The quicker they stop the better.

Love Songs

Rendered in a rich tenor voice
    Songs, so Neapolitan tender,
Serenading the ladies of nobility
    After going on a bender?

'Come Back To Sorrento'
    Is one of the famous four,
The melody lingering in the air
    Echoes from door to door.

'O Sole Mio' is another
    Not just an ice cream ad,
But a beautiful song
    Familiar to myriads.

'Santa Lucia' a saintly icon
    Praising a lady fair,
Setting as an example
    Virtue beyond compare.

'Catari, Catari' is the final one
    A gallant attempt at laud,
Think of a gentleman singer
    Brandishing his sword.

So these enchanting love songs
    Performed by many swains,
Have delighted their sweethearts
    Who heard them and heard again.

The Comfort of a Cat

Just a throbbing bundle of life
    Transmitting a purr,
This wonderful feline creature
    With its soft jet black fur.

So therapeutic to gently stroke
    And feel the cat's response,
He knows that I love him
    And of me he is fond.

He devours loads of cat sticks
    In all sorts of flavours,
I think the one he likes best
    Says rabbit on the label.

Soothing to my muddled head
    I feel I can relax,
When on my knee he sits
    With the comfort of a cat.

Once in a Time

Once in a time long ago
    When the world was young,
Mankind had only a toehold
    As onto life he clung.

Monsters huge prowled the earth
    Devouring all in sight,
Winged reptiles on the clifftops
    Were adept in their flight.

Man had only one saving craft
    He had a better brain,
He learned how to make tools
    And many beasts were slain.

Gradually, the beasts died out
    And man was left to forage,
Using his intellect to learn
    By strength, skill and courage.

Gathering food of fruit and plants
    He learned to cultivate grain,
So he slowly advanced
    With the help of sun and rain.

Reading and Romance

Many a maid reading a book
    Becomes beguiled, entranced,
Dreaming of what might have been
    Longing for romance.

She wants a knight protector
    Tricked out in full armour,
To sweep her off her feet
    She does not want a farmer.

She yearns for a nobleman
    As written in her books,
Tall, dark and charming
    Stunning in his looks.

She knows life is not like that
    She knows life is spartan,
She reads again, dreams again
    Of a Scots laird in his tartan.

There is nothing like the plaid
    And being in a clan,
Proud, noble, brave and tough
    Many a regal highland man.

She knows she would be lucky
    To find such a lad, it seems,
Especially quite handsome
    Perhaps, a lad of means.

Greetings Cards

An odd card at Christmas
    Maybe one for birthday,
Nothing the rest of the year
    Little to display.

The shelf has gathered dust
    Over more than thirty years
The old lady in the cottage
    Wipes away her tears.

Her family grown up and gone
    All many miles away,
She has tried to see them, but
    The taxi she cannot pay.

She longs for the phone to ring
    Or the post to bring a card,
Can she hear his footsteps
    Crossing the old farmyard?

Yes, it is the postman
    Who ignores the letterbox,
And sorts the mail in hand
    Then on the door he knocks.

There is a tied bundle
    That has to be signed for,
Excitedly she rips it open
    Finds greetings cards galore.

One a Day

Keith sits at his desk writing
    And with his pen does play,
Churning out reams of poetry
    At the rate of one a day.

The vast variety of subjects
    Covering each and all ideas,
Like the political rantings of
    Incompetent government and peers.

He thinks Britain's money
    Is being thrown away,
It should be kept here to free
    Britain from tyranny.

Each day he writes a poem
    Each day something new,
From this unique poet
    Who sees all points of view.

This truly remarkable writer
    Still writes one a day,
I hope posterity makes sure
    His work never fades away.

The Sty

Rooting about in the straw
    The pigs are in the sty,
Being fattened for the winter
    Without a reason why –

For they are a rare breed
    Gloucestershire Old Spots,
Valuable, alive and well
    The farmer knows what's what.

He's so canny a lad
    Whose family is Scots,
He will take great care
    Of Gloucestershire Old Spots.

Alas the farmer's wife
    Greedy, mean and sly,
Hates the thought of keeping
    Those pet pigs in the sty.

Funny how things turn out
    She has an itchy eye,
Rubbing only makes it worse
    She sports an angry stye.

The Tomboy

Climbing right to the top
    Savouring the sweet smell of hay,
The tomboy surveyed the scene
    And then flat out she lay.

Sleep came soft and swift
    She slept until sundown,
Awaking later she jumped
    Safely landing on the ground.

Time passed, once more she climbed
    With a farm boy on her arm,
Together, they soon cuddled up
    Hidden, high, safe from harm.

But not for very long
    For the rain began to pour,
And then her dress she tore
    Then it rained some more.

She scrambled down in haste
    Looking a shocking mess,
She dreaded telling her mother
    How she got a muddied dress.

In Time

We all secretly wish
    We could stop the rot of time,
Alas, it cannot be
    We're rapidly in decline.

From the moment of our birth
    Until we pop our clogs,
Our destiny always lies
    In the lap of the gods.

Is it all mapped out
    However hard we try?
'Tis said we have a choice
    That could be a lie.

Are we manipulated
    To suit a master plan,
That controls and directs
    The development of man?

Or is it that we believe
    That we alone define
Our lives and our destiny
    And all that comes in time?

Just Music?

You try to make a phone call
    And hear the music on hold,
Over and over again
    You are out in the cold.

There is no one there
    Just the pesky tape,
That loops round and round
    There seems no escape.

You become cross, then crosser
    And so terminate the call,
Holding on all that time
    Got you nowhere at all.

The telephone companies
    Gain from the music on hold,
They love the waiting time
    For them it's a mine of gold.

You have not made your call
    Your message you cannot send,
Why is it so damn hard?
    They just don't comprehend.

Lucky Numbers

'Tis said seven is a lucky number
    Will it win you the lottery?
There is an even greater treasure
    It's called the power of three.

This power can govern anything
    To which all is related,
From a clover leaf to deities
    In whose hands we are fated.

The trinity is now supreme
    Controlling the galaxies,
Proving that everything hinges
    On whims of power of three.

Stars, planets, comets, moons
    Empire satellites or free,
Including the earth, are subjugated
    In thrall to the power of three.

We cannot escape the stranglehold
    Of these mighty entities,
But in time we will understand
    The mighty power of three.

Sorcery

In a crooked cottage,
    Hidden deep in the woods
Lay a crone's book of spells,
    Next to a cape and hood.

She had a black familiar
    Constantly at her side,
That would gaze up on high
    When in the night she'd ride.

The priest in the village
    Was scared of the old crone,
His congregation dwindling
    Until he was left alone.

They kept creeping off
    To the cottage in the woods,
Leaving there their produce
    Exchanged for herbal goods.

The old woman's remedies
    From assorted plant life,
Administered on request
    To many a barren wife.

In time the wanted child arrived
    To a mother full of glee,
Gratefully, she gave thanks
    To this strange sorcery.

The Drifter

Each year, a little further
    The moon slow, drifts away,
Shattering ancient beliefs
    That it was here to stay.

The gravity of earth's pull
    Has a weakening hold,
The lunar orb's escaping
    Like a sheep from the fold.

What of the old creators?
    What is their mystic plan?
Will they, one day, return
    To protect ancient man –

From a terrible end
    Of natural disasters,
Earthquakes, floods and drought
    So say the forecasters.

But it need not be final
    The earthmen hold a clue,
The scientists may conspire
    And find out what to do.

The Harvest Field

Workers labour in the field
    Under the hot summer's sun.
Perspiring profusely, wishing
    Their day's work was done.

Sheaves of corn upright stand
    Like rows of little tents,
Shaped to shake off rain
    And rotting grain, prevents.

Long weeks out in the open
    'Til it's time to gather in,
Load the sheaves onto a cart
    Then home, the harvest bring.

The field is now bereft of crop
    Forlorn, bare and grim,
Winter through, it hibernates
    'Til the coming spring –

When the cycle starts again
    Another crop is drilled,
Not corn but with clover sweet
    The field once more fulfilled.

Regrets

There comes such moments in time
    We are bound to regret,
Maybe, a hurried romance
    Ending in a foolish step.

Why did we to the altar rush?
    Why did we make our vows?
A delay would have revealed
    Endless chain of rows.

Children should be blessings
    Alas 'tis not always so,
Trying to keep up with peers,
    Influences the way they grow.

Older folk are creatures of habit
    And often have cause to regret,
Refusing to be flexible
    No compromise is met.

By way of consolation
    We have animals to pet,
The love they give and comfort
    Are things we don't regret.

Redemption

'Tis said we all have sinned
    And so should seek redemption,
No matter which god we serve
    Conflicts, cause such tension.

High beings taught us many things
    From their places in the sky,
Going to war was one of them
    No rhyme nor reason why.

We carry this ancient flaw
    Preserved in our genes,
Were our teachers, known as gods
    Sent in friendship or fiends?

They gave us curiosity
    To question as a whole,
We believe their motive
    Was absolute control.

To manipulate, pull and drive
    Forcing us to learn,
Only time will help us
    To deal with their return.

Ancestors

It is very difficult
    To trace your ancient bloodline,
The further back you go
    More branches you find.

There could be many kinds of kin
    From yeomen to lords,
Highwaymen to actors
    Nightly treading the boards.

Who knows, maybe Vikings
    Normans with the Duke,
Carriers of rich blue blood
    Found Saxon ladies to suit.

There could be saints or sinners
    It is exciting to find,
Through records down the ages
    Your very own bloodline.

Dimensions

Split, only seconds apart
    Yet, almost identical,
Occupying near space
    Time incomprehensible.

Will events turn out alike?
    Within each dimension,
Maybe, rulers of such kingdoms
    Have similar intentions.

If there's a galactic war
    Who would sport the crown?
For to the winner goes all
    Be he clever or a clown.

Close in time the dimensions,
    Unknown energies at work,
Diverse one from the other
    In timeless distance lurk.

In the end does it matter
    What reveals the dimensions?
If there's an aged formula
    Leave to wise comprehension.

Dead or Alive

Certain posters displayed
    Said wanted dead or alive,
With reward for their capture
    So very few survived.

Some did elude the law
    Some were not guilty,
Needing support of friends
    Relying on their loyalty.

Many were tracked by lawmen
    Out to seek revenge,
For crimes in their county
    They wanted to avenge.

Mainly it was decided
    When all was said and done,
Whether lawman or outlaw
    It was the fastest gun.

Earthbound

When violent crime's committed
    Quite often 'tis found,
The spirit can't pass over
    And so remains earthbound.

Properties can bind it
    And thus not set it free,
Death repeats for some
    Others, fearful be.

Spirits do not want to haunt
    Or visit former scenes,
They really have no choice
    They're trapped in-between –

Existing as a phantom
    In ghostly realms are bound,
If from limbo they escape
    They go without a sound.

Lady Fox

She trots into our garden
    A pretty lady fox,
Sniffing along the ground
    Black nose and matching socks.

A large sweeping brush
    So red, thick and warm
Her russet, silky coat
    Paler when first born.

We put out titbits nightly
    She chooses first the best,
Part of the dog's dinner
    Later she eats the rest.

Halfway down the garden
    Trotting back to her den,
She turns and looks back
    And will return again.

Does she have cubs
    Waiting anxiously?
Hoping they will be joined
    By their dog fox daddy.

Dew Under the Sun

Destined never to linger
    Is dew under the sun,
Moistures all the plants
    For moments, then 'tis gone.

Is it the same with human life?
    We have so short a span,
Have we been modified
    To suit an alien plan?

If we are in their mould
    Then why leave out a gene,
Did they just need us
    To be a work machine?

It seems that after aeons
    Before work was done,
There came a time the masters
    Left, their control now gone.

Slow, our species plodded on
    Never learning to run,
Living but a little while
    Like the dew under the sun.

A Parcel

Children find it exciting
    When a parcel's at the door,
Even though they don't know
    Exactly who it's for.

Is it for their mother
    From a mail-order store?
To be stuffed in a wardrobe
    That can't hold any more.

Maybe it's for their father
    Bought from abroad,
A civil war pistol
    To be shown with his sword.

When the wrapping is torn off
    Inside there's a box,
Containing non-exciting
    Auntie's diabetic socks.

Remnants

Are we just the leftovers
    Mainly only bits and bobs,
Or did our earth arise
    From wars between the gods –

Who destroyed the galaxy
    And left our solar system
As floating rocks in space,
    Devoid of life and wisdom.

From such destruction
    Form'd, third from the sun
A world from out of chaos
    Earth's creation had begun –

And in time this green orb
    With land and water to share,
Gave birth to diverse life
    With breath of new fresh air.

That left the lifeless ones
    Remnants still revolving,
Will they turn out to be
    New worlds, late evolving?

Summer Snow

One thing that is certain
    Just as night follows day,
A fall of snow in summer
    Will not hang around nor stay.

Looking like dust on the ground,
    Is it trouble ahead,
Sign of a bad harvest
    So folklore has said.

Snow in summer is rare
    Unnatural a climate,
Sprouting of green shoots
    Will be slow and late.

It is unusual
    For snow in summertime,
Quite out of season
    Nature's thus unkind.

The reverse is true in December
    A carpet of protective snow,
Bulbs and roots so shielded
    In spring will surely grow.

Lollipop Lady

Standing on the pathway
    Small in stature, big in heart,
Near the school crossing
    She daily plays her part.

Stepping out into the road
    Holding up the cars,
Her banner on a pole
    All moving traffic, bars.

Children then cross the road
    As they do every day,
After nine o'clock
    She scurries well away.

Some mothers stay to gossip
    And their cars block the road,
Angry motorists hoot and
    Tempers soon explode.

The lollipop lady returns
    In sunshine or in rain,
Helping all the children
    To cross the road again.

Eyes

Organs sited in the head
    Able to see near and far,
From minute microdots
    To a twinkling of a star.

It's a wonderful function
    This great gift of sight,
There are some without it
    Their lives dark as night.

Men of science aid their vision
    With powerful telescopes,
Charting heavenly bodies
    In space so remote.

There are rare birds in nature
    Who on eyesight do rely,
Such as hawks and falcons
    Predators of the skies.

We can see in full colour
    Many animals cannot,
We should be grateful, our eyes
    Distinguish such a lot.

Moon Watch

We gaze at the moon and wonder
    What strange shadows we see,
'Tis said the moon has power
    To control fertility.

The tides on this island earth
    To and fro are pulled,
By earth's single satellite
    In wane and wax are ruled.

The mystery of this orb
    Imagination fires
Viewers worldwide over
    All wonder and admire.

The nearest object in space
    Where man on moon has walked,
Were the Apollo missions
    In secrecy wrought.

Pipes and Drums

No greater sound can be heard
    Than dramatic pipes and drums,
The march of Scottish regiments
    Just sheer magic it becomes.

Entering the parade ground
    Sporting their tartan dress,
Swishing in their movements
    These soldiers always impress –

Whoever hears the music swell
    To a final crescendo,
The pipes skirling the high notes
    Drums beating out the low.

Marching into battle
    As heard in days of old,
The regimental band
    The very heart and soul.

Newspapers

I love papers that inform
    That which is going on,
The doings of famous people
    And battles fought and won.

Publications of diverse size
    From tabloid to broadsheet,
Some are just black and white
    Colour, an occasional treat.

Some are politically biased
    Many have things to buy,
Others have columns of notices
    Of born, married and died.

In February each year
    They publish valentines,
Simple to complex messages
    A most romantic time.

If you really want notoriety
    You're mentioned in *The Times*,
Featured on one of its many pages
    As either sordid or sublime.

The Bridge

I see the fishes swimming
    As on the bridge I stand,
A little wider than most
    It links land to land.

Right in the very middle
    Giving me the shivers,
An ancient chapel is there
    Hanging over the river.

What tales it could tell
    This medieval arch,
Days of old, servants sold
    Driven by the Church –

A prime example
    Of their hypocrisy,
They should humbly practice
    Christian charity.

So, the river continues
    Flowing under the bridge,
Nourishing the stagnant pools
    That's home to weed and midge.

Sunblock

The sun glare is on the screen
    A pity to shut it out,
But I can't see a thing,
    Just shadows that dance about.

Now I can see the movie
    For the room's now in shade,
But the sun behind the curtains
    Just causes them to fade.

While the sun on glass behind
    With such powerful rays,
Focusing on one point
    Could shortly cause a blaze.

And fair hair and skin type
    Detests the direct sun,
Some may sunbathe for hours
    Cooking, until they're done.

Nations of a different kind
    Where sun shines all the year,
Do not need a sunblock
    They are protected it appears.

Stepping Stones

As an aid to crossing water
    Placed across a stream,
People jumped stone to stone
    With caution it would seem.

So easy to slip and fall
    On stones slimy set,
Many an unlucky person
    Was soon soaking wet.

The water was quite shallow
    And hidden under the stones.
Nature's diverse wildlife
    Found this place their home.

It was thus well known
    When a lady crossed the stream,
Reflected in the water
    Her legs could be seen.

On the banks of the stream
    Like a row of clones,
Cattle slaked their thirst
    Away from stepping stones.

The Thatcher

A great asset to the village
    Is this craftsman of skill,
Repairing cottage roofs
    That have holes to fill.

Using local materials
    Like long wheat straw,
Holding to a basic charge
    As folk cannot pay more.

He has a young village lad
    To yawmin up the load,
Where he spreads it safely
    With tidy ends that showed.

This helps the rain run down
    And does not soak in,
A medieval custom
    Handed down to him –

By his father, who found
    That the Norfolk reed,
Lasted much longer, and
    Perfect for every need.

The Milestone

Standing at the crossroads
    Erected long ago,
The milestone indicates
    Distances to and fro.

For those who cannot read
    Their fingers can feel,
Finding information
    The ancient stone reveals.

Robbers on the run
    Often turned the stone around,
Aiding their escape, hoping
    To muddle and confound.

A focal point for travellers
    Confirming where and place,
An ideal spot perhaps
    For refreshments to taste.

Lord of the Manor

Lord of the manor house
    Yet he lives there alone,
Once, it bustled with people
    With the family at home.

His ancestors once dwelt there
    A long line of lords,
With a team of servants
    And a good life was assured.

Sorely missing his parents
    His sisters and brothers,
Victims of the plague that
    Wiped out many others.

Close to, in the village
    There lives a pretty maid,
Daughter of the blacksmith
    Who helps there unpaid.

Her face and clothes are smudged
    As she pets a turtle dove,
And the lord of the manor
    Knows, she is his one true love.

But he is painfully aware
    Of his rank and station,
Yet wedding this lowly lass,
    Will end his isolation.

Diverse Arts

A comprehensive genre
    Men of every art,
Poets, composers, inventors
    Players of diverse arts.

They have one thing in common
    Hardship through poverty,
Causing much deprivation
    As nothing is really free.

Many paid a high price
    Sickness dogged their lives,
Slowing down their work for
    They were barely alive.

But out of years of illness
    Emerged despite the pain,
Such grand art and inventions
    Like the Spitfire and *The Hay Wain*.

Used Cars Salesman

Is he to be trusted
    This seller of wheels?
Many people doubt it
    And shop around for deals.

His stock may seem attractive
    But he offers no guarantee,
Customers hope, if they buy
    A car, will it pass the MOT.

Glossy and shiny the bodywork
    The engine looks rust free,
Will it start when wanted
    Or have a flat battery?

Cars parked on his outside lot
    Arranged to catch the eye,
It's blatantly obvious
    That his prices are too high.

He prefers to deal in cash
    Avoiding part exchange,
Yet, when the taxman calls round
    His confidence soon wanes –

For he knows he has to show
    His cash kept in a box,
Hoping he will be spared
    When he opens the lock.

The Wheelwright

A well-known local craftsman
    The thatcher's elder brother,
Worked by the village pond
    Watched over by his mother –

Who had a habit of nagging,
    Driving his father wild,
Until the day he grabbed his hat
    And storm'd away, full riled.

He learned his skill by watching
    His father work on the wheel,
Wooden spokes and hot iron rim
    Together to be sealed.

When bound and cooled
    There was a lasting bond,
Achieved by swelling the wood
    In the shallow village pond.

A great asset for local folk,
    He fixed their broken carts,
Making no charge for repairs
    Out of goodness of his heart.

The Old Carpenter

He has a dusty workshop
    Full of benches, pots and tools,
He makes chairs and tables
    And farmers' milking stools.

He is a craftsman of
    Ancient heritage and true,
Said to be a descendant
    Of blue blood, 'til war ensued.

Very much in demand
    As his standard is high,
He's never short of work
    And always occupied.

He has it in his head
    To make a bedside chair,
A gift for his lovely cousin
    Whose bed he aims to share.

The Old Shopkeeper

Stocking assorted wares for sale
    The village shop sold day to day,
Basic needs for village folk
    Come weather or what may.

Butter, cheese, milk and eggs
    All from farms nearby,
Choice ham and fresh bacon from pigs
    Home-made, succulent pies.

His shop a centre of gossip
    Where housewives gather to chat,
Scandals, births, deaths, marriages
    They stand and chew the fat.

Outside are wooden posts
    For tethering dogs or a horse,
Animals wait, for their owners
    To emerge in due course.

He listens to village talk
    And has for many years,
Understanding their problems
    Lives, hopes and fears.

The Village Ironmonger

His shopfront boasts hardware
    Buckets, pots, saucepans,
Inside, candles, paraffin and coal
    Assorted paints in cans.

Nails, screws in little drawers
    Nuts, bolts and locks,
Goods lined upon shelves
    And brackets in a box.

A valued part of rural life
    His prices pitched quite low,
His shop next to the pub made
    Some folk stumble to and fro.

Outside the shop, 'gainst the wall
    Leant shovels, forks and spades,
Rakes and hoes, new barrows
    Lined the entrance way.

In a corner, the china,
    Cups, teapots, plates and more,
A veritable display
    In this well-run store.

Agricultural Merchants

Occupying a large plot of land
    The farmers' friend to heed,
Sold machinery, diverse types
    Depending on the need.

Tractors, combine harvesters
    Standing in huge sheds,
Protected from the weather
    And painted yellow or red.

These large giants of the land
    Are never purchased cheap,
Farmers hope, in harvest time,
    They will earn their keep.

No longer pulled by horses
    The ploughs, scuffles or discs,
Are pulled by tractors now,
    Though, wider land strips miss.

Imported tractors, 'n' implements
    Agricultural merchants know,
To own expensive machinery
    You need a larger loan.

The Chemist

He is a man of science
    His shop a multi display,
Of shiny, big glass bottles
    In colourful array.

With many a medical pill
    Balm for diverse aches and pains,
So good are his products
    No trace of ache remains.

Mothers seek baby food
    The best for their child,
Sold in little jars
    Bland and very mild.

Some young lass in trouble
    Would try to enlist his aid,
He's just not allowed, to dispense
    The poison that's forbade.

Bandages, sticking plasters
    Ointments, are his wares,
All direct remedies
    Cuts 'n' bruises to repair.

A farmer comes with bloated gut
    He's drunk too much beer,
Down the hatch with peppermint!
    And his problem soon will clear.

Internet Banking

It may seem convenient
    But is your data intact?
Payments flow out
    It's a worrying fact.

You may appear protected
    With diverse secret codes,
But crooks experiment
    The nasty little toads.

However, any decent bank
    Will spot the wrong amount,
They'll run a check and refund
    Back into your account –

Payments taken wrongly,
    In just a few working days,
My money is now returned
    And I hope this time it stays!

So, what of interest
    Your money would have earned?
Well, that's gone for good
    A hard lesson learned.